The Dream Compass

Using Dreams as Your Guide

Hitomi Sakamoto, PhD

Published by BookLocker.com, Inc., St. Petersburg, Florida.

Printed on acid-free paper.

BookLocker.com, Inc.
2018

First Edition

Illustrations by Silvana Oprea

DISCLAIMER

This book details the author's personal experiences with and opinions about dream interpretation and dreamwork. The author is not a licensed medical professional.

The author and publisher are providing this book and its contents on an "as is" basis and make no representations or warranties of any kind with respect to this book or its contents. The author and publisher disclaim all such representations and warranties, including for example warranties of merchantability, dream interpretation, psychology and self-help advice for a particular purpose. In addition, the author and publisher do not represent or warrant that the information accessible via this book is accurate, complete or current.

The statements made about products and services have not been evaluated by the U.S. government. Please consult with your own legal, accounting, medical, or other licensed professional regarding the suggestions and recommendations made in this book.

Except as specifically stated in this book, neither the author or publisher, nor any authors, contributors, or other representatives will be liable for damages arising out of or in connection with the use of this book. This is a comprehensive limitation of liability that applies to all damages of any kind, including (without limitation) compensatory; direct, indirect or consequential damages; loss of data, income or profit; loss of or damage to property and claims of third parties.

You understand that this book is not intended as a substitute for consultation with a licensed medical, legal or accounting professional. Before you begin any change your lifestyle in any way, you will consult a licensed professional to ensure that you are doing what's best for your situation.

This book provides content related to dream interpretation and personal development. As such, use of this book implies your acceptance of this disclaimer.

For my parents

Acknowledgments

I would like to thank my partner and co-organizer of Dream Cafe, Adi Andrei, for inspiring me to write this book, supporting me every step of the way, creating some of the dreamwork methods, and ensuring I completed the project. I pay tribute to my teachers of dreamwork, especially Drs. Arnold and Amy Mindell and their colleagues at Process Work Institute in Portland, Oregon. Many of the methods in this book are inspired by what I learned from them. My heartfelt thanks go out to all my friends, colleagues and family members for their encouragement and support, and to all my workshop participants, including Dream Cafe group members, for their openness to trying out new methods with me. Finally, special thanks to Silvana Oprea for creating beautiful illustrations for the book, and to my wonderful editor, Olivia Shannon.

Table of Contents

Introduction

Dreams are treasure troves of messages, ideas and information. They teach us how to see things differently, solve problems in new ways, find our inner potential and develop our creativity. Just as compasses guide explorers through unknown terrain, dreams can guide us through life's challenges.

I wrote **The Dream Compass: Using Dreams as Your Guide** in the hope of showing you how your dreams can help you navigate the journey of life. In my twenty-four years as a psychotherapist, I have helped decipher the hidden meanings of thousands of dreams. I have discovered that it is important to know where to focus your attention when interpreting dreams, and I have identified a few basic steps to dream interpretation that are easy and fun to learn. Throughout the book, I will introduce you to dreamwork methods I have used to help people around the world. Through a range of examples, tips and exercises, I will help you bridge the gap between your nighttime experiences and everyday life.

This book will help you remember your dreams, find the right attitude for exploring dreams, interpret dream messages, and use the wisdom of your dreams to help with your life direction and self-development. You will notice that this is not a dream dictionary; that is, I do not focus on assigning set meanings to dream symbols. Instead, my goal is to help you find the personal meanings of dream images.

The first few chapters introduce you to the basics of dream interpretation. If you are looking to start interpreting your dreams right away, jump to Chapter 5. Chapter 13 includes a summary of all the dreamwork methods. The List of Common Dream Themes in Appendix B goes through some common dream images that have universal meanings for almost everyone.

I believe understanding nighttime dreams is as essential to your well-being as taking good care of your physical body is. I hope this book will help you navigate your dream world and bring back many friendly messages and magical treasures.

Hitomi Sakamoto
London, U.K.
January 2018

Before You Start...

Please make sure to read the following before you begin:

- ❖ It's always a good idea to balance your waking life and dream life. If you feel upset, unbalanced or confused after exploring your dreams, stop looking into them for a while. Check to see if you have been taking care of yourself physically. For example, have you been eating balanced meals? Resting enough? Exercising regularly? Take action where necessary. You can go back to working with dreams when you feel ready.

- ❖ Don't worry if you don't remember or stop remembering dreams. If that happens, maybe it's time to focus on your daytime activities.

- ❖ Dreamwork is not meant to replace standard medical or psychotherapy treatment or any emergency procedure. Please seek professional help if you are suffering from severe mental distress or confusion, experiencing sudden and severe physical symptoms, or dealing with a serious issue that puts you or others in danger in some way.

Map of The Dream Compass: How to Use This Book

❖ **If you want to take your time to enjoy exploring the dream world:**
→ Start from *Chapter 1*

❖ **If you want to start learning the dreamwork method right away:**
→ Jump to *Chapter 5*

❖ **If you want to know "How to Use Dreams as Your Guide" in a nutshell:**
→ Go to Appendix C or *Chapter 13*

Chapter 1
Making Friends with Your Dreams

When you have an amazing dream, strange dream, scary dream, or mysterious dream, what do you do? Do you pay attention to it? Talk to someone about it?

Dreams can be fascinating, with curious characters and strange events. You may suddenly find yourself flying through the air, being chased by a monster, or landing on a beautiful island with extraordinary plants and animals you have never seen in waking life. Are they just meaningless illusions that the mind creates during the night, or do they actually mean something?

For example, my friend Olivia, a teacher, told me about the following dream she had:

** Olivia's Dream **

"I was supposed to be an actress in a theater company in this dream. All of a sudden, I was behind the curtain on a stage, and very soon I would have to go out there and say my lines. I felt a little panicky, as I had no idea what I was supposed to say. When the curtain went up, I saw that it was a full house. To my surprise, the words just flowed out of my mouth, and the show was a great success."

Did Olivia's dream have any special meaning for her? Yes! As we explored the dream, she started to make connections between what she was experiencing in the dream and her everyday life. Did the dream mean she was stressed or wanting more attention? These were possibilities. However, as you will see in the next chapter, she found that the meaning of her dream went much deeper. The dream pointed her in a new direction in her life.

You, too, will be able to understand the meaning of your dreams like Olivia did. I'm going to show you how to decode the meanings of each dream part, put them all together and build a bridge between dream messages and your waking life.

It's useful to imagine that nighttime dreams are like messengers from a faraway land. Sometimes it's not easy to notice them because they are a little shy, and sometimes you ignore them because you are busy with your everyday routine. The good news is, dreams are very patient and will keep knocking on your door until the messages get delivered. When you don't open the door for a long time, the knocks get louder and louder. That's when you have the same kind of dreams over and over, or when you have an intense dream that makes you jump out of bed.

It's time to answer the door and start making friends with your dreams. Here are a few tips for making better connections with them:

- ❖ Have a special notebook and pen or a voice recorder ready at your bedside.
- ❖ Before falling asleep, set the intention that you will remember dreams if they have important messages

for you. Just say in your mind, "I will remember my dreams when I wake up."

❖ When you wake up, without moving your body, try drifting your awareness back to your dream.

❖ Record your dreams while you are still lying down. Try not to write in perfect sentences. Sometimes it's better to jot down a few words, feelings or atmospheres. You could also sketch a few images.

❖ People tend to find it easier to remember dreams when they awake naturally, without an alarm. Consider trying the above method the next time you don't have any plans in the morning.

Don't worry if you can't remember any dreams at first. You don't have to catch every single dream. Sometimes it's great to enjoy a deep sleep without remembering any dreams. As I mentioned earlier, important dreams will knock on your door again and again anyway.

In the next chapter, you will learn more about how to welcome your dreams and how to begin to understand their messages.

Next time you have an interesting dream, try talking to someone. Ask them if they have had any interesting dreams lately.

Chapter 2
Feeling Your Way into the Dream World

In the previous chapter, we learned that dreams are like messengers from a faraway land. They speak in an unfamiliar language, and their messages may seem vague or riddle-like. When you listen to them, try to slow down, be open-minded and use your imagination.

Olivia's Dream

Let's look at Olivia's dream from Chapter 1 and try listening to what it has to say. Try to feel into the special quality and atmosphere of the dream.

> ..."I was supposed to be an actress in a theater company in this dream. All of a sudden, I was behind the curtain on a stage, and very soon I would have to go out there and say my lines. I felt a little panicky, as I had no idea what I was supposed to say. When the curtain went up, I saw that it was a full house. To my surprise, the words just flowed out of my mouth, and the show was a great success."

Olivia was a teacher in real life. However, in her dream she was all of a sudden on the stage as an actress. Can you feel the anxiety she might have felt as she waited for the curtain to rise in the semidarkness? Then the curtain went up, and the next thing she knew, she was in the spotlight. In front of her was a wide space, and she was facing all the people watching her. For some mysterious reason, once she was in front of the audience, she knew exactly what to say, and the show was a great success. What a relief! But what does it all mean?

The first thing to remember is that **dream messages are expressed in symbols and metaphors.** Instead of saying, "You need to take a break," a dream may show you an image of a tropical island. Instead of saying, "You should change how you deal with things," a dream might show you moving to a different town.

You can often guess what a dream image means by asking yourself, "What could it symbolize?"

Olivia was able to discover, after using the creative dreamwork method described in Chapter 5 of this book, that the image of

  "her being an actress"

was a symbol for

  "her own self-expression and creativity."

The meaning of the image of

"words flowing out of her mouth"

was in fact about

"being spontaneous and going with the flow."

To put it all together, the dream was saying something like this:

> Olivia has the potential to be more expressive and creative (actress) as well as to be more spontaneous and go with the flow (words flowing out of her mouth). Embracing this side of herself may work very well for her, and may be well-received (large audience; the show was a great success).

In short, the dream's message for Olivia was that it was time for her to start paying attention to her own creativity and spontaneity. Based on the dream message, she decided to make a few changes in her life. She started taking watercolor painting lessons, which she had always wanted to do. She also tried to go with the flow when she was teaching her class. If she suddenly had a good idea about how to teach a certain subject, she would try it, even if it was different from what she had planned. You know what? Her students loved it!

Don't worry if you find it difficult to interpret dreams at first. I will show you how to decode the messages of your dreams using simple and fun exercises. The important thing is, when you try to understand your dreams, you need to slow down a little and let go of any preconceived ideas.

Creating a Space for Your Dreams

It's always a good idea to create a quiet space in your mind when you try to remember a dream or explore its meaning. This is also a way of honoring your dreams. Take a couple of deep breaths and maybe close your eyes before starting to interpret your dreams so that you can appreciate their special qualities.

** Creating a Welcoming Space for Your Dreams **

1) Sit comfortably and take a few deep breaths. With each exhale, imagine any thoughts or noise in your head melting away.
2) Think of a safe space where you feel absolutely comfortable. What is the space like? It may be an imaginary room, a peaceful place in nature or a space full of light.
3) Imagine you are in that space. Keep on breathing. Feel how relaxed and safe you are in this space.

When you slow down and create an open space in yourself like this, you may find that you suddenly start to remember not only dreams, but also something important you've forgotten, or you may have great ideas and solutions to problems popping into your head. Try doing this exercise anytime you have a minute to spare, like when you are riding a bus or waiting in line in a store.

Before you go to bed, try closing your eyes and breathing out memories of the day's experiences and thoughts in your head one by one, until you feel your mind is fairly empty.

Chapter 3
Different Types of Dreams

During sleep, the radar of your consciousness expands as your mind relaxes, allowing you to access information that your waking mind cannot process on its own. Dreams translate this information into images and stories that serve many purposes. In this chapter I give an overview of several different types of dreams, based on their functions and characteristics. Of course, many dreams have multiple purposes that transcend such categorization, but classifying dreams can be a useful way to get started.

** Dream Categories **

- ❖ Space-Cleaner Dreams
- ❖ Insight-into-Situation Dreams
- ❖ Premonition Dreams
- ❖ Your-Inner-World Dreams
- ❖ Special-Experience Dreams
- ❖ Direct-Message Dreams
- ❖ Lucid Dreams
- ❖ Recurring Dreams
- ❖ Dreams for Your Community

---

1. Space-Cleaner Dreams

What I call **Space-Cleaner Dreams** are the ones where you view scenes from your life or go over thoughts you had during the day. In these dreams, you simply relive your waking thoughts and experiences. Not much else is going on. You often have this kind of dream right after you fall asleep, especially if you were doing something that kept your mind busy, such as watching television, reading a book or worrying. Your subconscious may be sorting memories and thoughts, perhaps even throwing them away to clear space for more important information to come in later dreams.

2. Insight-into-Situation Dreams

Many dreams give you insight into situations in your life. For example, Tim, a friend of mine, was having difficulty deciding between two job offers. Although Company A offered him a slightly larger salary, there was something about Company B that kept him from accepting Company A's offer. One day Tim dreamed he was visiting each company's office, one after the other. Company A's office was cold, dark and empty, with no windows. Company B's office not only had windows and was full of light, but also had people smiling at him.

When he awoke, Tim reflected on his real-life experiences visiting each company. He suddenly remembered that Company B's office had a lively energy with employees who seemed happy, while Company A's office had a cold atmosphere that made him tense and tired. He decided to go for Company B despite the smaller salary. He realized he would be happiest working in a cheerful atmosphere with upbeat colleagues. Besides, he reasoned, Company B had the potential to pay him a higher salary in the future.

Tim's dream gave him insight into a situation that his waking mind struggled to understand on its own. The dream helped him reflect on the situation from a new perspective, and it helped him make the final decision.

You may also have dreams where you in your dream have different emotional reactions from usual to certain people or situations. These dreams are encouraging you to be aware of your feelings for them that you haven't been conscious of.

3. Premonition Dreams

Many people have reported experiencing events in waking life that their dreams had already shown them. It appears that the expanded consciousness of the dream state sometimes enables people to catch a glimpse of future possibilities. However, if you have a bad dream that seems to be about a future event, don't worry. The future is not set in stone. Chances are, the dream is trying to show you one of the *possible* outcomes, based on what is currently happening in your life. You have the opportunity to reflect on the dream and pay attention to the way you are dealing with the situation, thus changing the outcome.

This is what happened to Debbie. She dreamed she was driving in a town she had never visited in waking life. She was distracted by a group of teenagers who were making a lot of noise, and she crashed into another car.

A week later, Debbie's company sent her on a business trip. To her surprise, she found herself driving in a town that looked eerily similar to the town in her dream. Soon she saw a large group of teenagers who were shouting and throwing things at each other. Remembering her dream, she focused on her driving and tried not to be distracted, and she managed to drive home safely.

Debbie's premonition dream showed her a possible future if she allowed herself to become distracted while driving.

She learned from the dream and prevented a possible car accident.

4. Your-Inner-World Dreams

Dreams often use different characters and stories to teach you about yourself. By looking into such dreams, you can get a map of your inner world—including the parts of yourself that you don't know so much about.

For example, Olivia's dream about being an actress, discussed in Chapter 1, was about her inner world. The dream was inviting her to recognize the side of herself she didn't really know; that is, the creative and expressive Olivia who was more spontaneous and could go with the flow.

Many dreams, especially the ones that leave you with lingering impressions, are encouraging you to learn more about yourself, especially your potential. Your potential is a latent aspect that exists within yourself, but has not yet manifested in everyday life. Like a muscle you have never used, your potential is waiting to be developed. **Your-Inner-World Dreams** help you become more aware of your potential. Helping us learn about ourselves may be one of the most important functions of nighttime dreams. As you stretch yourself and start using those "unused muscles," you will become stronger and find it easier to navigate life with more flow, meaning and purpose.

In the next chapters, we will mainly focus on Your-Inner-World Dreams. You may be surprised to discover that even the scariest and darkest dreams actually have positive and important meanings for you.

5. Special-Experience Dreams

These dreams leave you with special feelings or inner experiences that are more significant than the actual contents of the dream. In fact, the experiences can be so strong that interpretation is often unnecessary.

I had such a dream after my father passed away. A few days after his death, I had a dream that my father was very happy. He had the most beautiful smile on his face. In the dream and even after I woke up, I had a joyful and almost blissful feeling in my heart that stayed with me for a long time and helped me cope with the grief. Dreams like this one seem to be there just to help us have certain feelings, or what some people might call "spiritual experiences."

6. Direct-Message Dreams

What I call **Direct-Message Dreams** are the ones in which you hear, see or sense clear messages that do not need much interpretation. These messages are supportive, educational or instructive. For example, Yoko, who had a tendency to work too hard as an accountant of a big firm, was suffering from chronic fatigue. One night she dreamed of a sign on her kitchen wall that said:

"STOP WORKING SO HARD AND TAKE A REST"

The message of this dream was clear and obvious: It was time for Yoko to take a break.

Likewise, some dreams offer direct answers to our questions. A patient of mine was once struggling with algebra homework. He gave up and went to sleep. In the dream he saw an answer written in his notebook. When he awoke, he checked it to find it was correct.

Of course, I'm not saying you should blindly follow such messages in your dreams. However, when you do have a dream that seems to contain a direct message for you, it's always worth considering whether it has any relevance to your life situations.

7. Lucid Dreams

Have you ever had a dream where you knew you were dreaming? These are called **Lucid Dreams,** and many people have experienced them. There are books that describe ways to induce and sustain lucid dreams, but that is beyond the scope of this book. However, I can tell you one thing about lucid dreams: They can also be interpreted as Your-Inner-World-Dreams. Lucid dreams can help you with your self-development by giving insight into your inner potential.

8. Recurring Dreams

This is not exactly a specific type of dream, but many people tell me they have the same dreams over and over again. Others report having dreams that are slightly different from each other, but with the same themes. Why is it that some people have recurring dreams? As I explained earlier, dreams have important information and messages for you. If you don't notice these messages, the same dreams will keep on knocking on your door until you start paying attention to them.

For example, Tia, a member of Dream Cafe, told me she had decided to join the group because she had been regularly having the same dream for almost twenty-five years. After working with us, she finally came to understand her dream's message. She started taking actions based on its wisdom, and within a few weeks, she had stopped having the recurring dream.

9. Dreams for Your Community

It might be possible for the expanded consciousness of the dreaming self to reach beyond the personal sphere and tap into information for the collective. This would explain why people sometimes feel their dreams contain messages for others or for humanity in general.

For example, sharing dreams and understanding their meaning is central for the life of the Achuar, an indigenous tribe living in the rainforest of Ecuador. The Achuar believe some dreams have messages for the community, and they take action based on the futures predicted by these dreams.

In the early '90s, the Achuar elders and shamans started having shared dreams of an imminent threat to their land. In response, the Achuar clans began joining forces, organizing themselves into The Achuar Federation. Together they began seeking partnership with neighboring tribes, and they discovered an oil development in the Amazon was about to destroy the rainforest and their traditional way of life. Luckily, the Achuar were ready to meet this threat: The now-united group decided to seek help from activists from the modern world. By working together, the Achuar have been able to protect their land and preserve their culture—and all because they listened to the wisdom of their dreams.

* * *

In this chapter we have briefly explored several types of dreams. Note that some dreams can belong to more than one category. For example, Debbie had a **Premonition Dream** about driving in a new town and seeing a group of loud teenagers. At the same time, it would have been interesting if she had explored this dream as an **Inner-**

World Dream. She may then have discovered her inner teenager who yearned to be more vocal and fun-loving.

Chapter 4
Interpreting Dream Images (1)

So far you've learned how to make better friends with your dreams, how to create a space in yourself to welcome and honor them, and how to differentiate them by their characteristics and functions. Now you are ready to move on to the basics of dream interpretation.

Dream Messages Come in Symbols

Remember I said dreams use symbols and analogies when sending you messages? A symbol is something that stands for something else. That's why it often doesn't work so well to take dreams literally.

For example, let's pretend you had a dream that *"someone gave you a delicious-looking cake."*

You may already be guessing that the dream would not be about an actual cake. You are right!

24

Meaning of a Dream Symbol is Unique for Everyone

What, then, is the dream trying to tell you by showing you a cake? An important point to remember about dream interpretation is that the meaning of a dream symbol is often personal and unique to you. In other words, the same dream image can have a different meaning for someone else.

Try the following exercise to find out what "a delicious-looking cake" could symbolize for you.

** Symbolic Meaning of a Cake **

1) Close your eyes and take a few deep breaths. You can also do the "Creating a Welcoming Space" exercise from Chapter 2.
2) Now imagine a cake. Any kind of cake. Don't think too much. Just let one pop into your mind.
3) What does it look like? Notice if there is something special about it.
4) What is its special quality? How is it different from all other cakes? What makes it stand out? If the cake has a unique power, what would it be?

The answers to the last questions would be the actual meaning of the symbol "cake" for you at this moment. For example, my friend Jan imagined a cake with lots of colorful candies on top. When I asked about the cake's special quality and unique power, she said that:

*"The cake has a **playful** quality and the power to make people **happy**."*

For Jan, the particular cake she imaged was a symbol for **"playfulness and happiness."**

If Jan had a dream that someone gave her this colorful cake, the meaning of the dream could be that "it's important to pay attention to something about playfulness and happiness." Since the dream is about someone giving her the cake, which means it's somehow "approaching her," you could word the dream interpretations in the following ways:

❖ Something playful and happy (it could be feelings or events) is coming her way.

❖ She needs to give herself more of what makes her feel playful and happy.

❖ She has a playful and happy side of herself that she may not know so much about, and she may want to embrace it more.

But which was the correct meaning for Jan?

There is No Correct Answer with Dream Interpretation

When it comes to dream interpretation, there is no one correct answer. The important thing is whether the message resonates with the dreamer and she finds it useful for her life and the situations in which she finds herself.

We asked Jan which of the possible dream meanings felt most right for her. She chose the second message. She said she had been so busy taking care of her family, she often forgot to take care of herself. The idea of giving herself time and care so that she could have playful and happy feelings sounded like a very important message for her.

You might say, "But it wasn't a real dream, just an imaginary cake!"

As we discussed at the end of Chapter 2, dreams are only one avenue through which important information and messages arrive to you. When you make yourself dreamy and let your imagination take over, what comes up is like a daydream, and it has messages for you that are just as important.

What is the message of an imaginary cake for you?

** Dream Decoding Exercise **

Using the steps outlined above, think of what special qualities the following dream images have for you:

Dream Image	Example of Its Characteristics or Energy
A Dog	friendly, fun-loving, playful, etc.
Dark night	very peaceful and quiet, mysterious, etc.
Your next door neighbor	serious, artistic, kind, etc.
(your dream image:)	

Don't worry if you find it difficult. We'll practice more in the following chapters, and pretty soon you'll get the hang of it.

Common Themes in Dreams

I have good news for you. Although I mentioned that the meanings of dream images are often personal and unique to you, there are other dream images and symbols that are more universal. These images have the same meanings for almost everyone. If your dream contains universally shared images, then you may not need to go through the steps above. Using the List of Common Dream Themes in Appendix B, you may quickly interpret the meanings of some dream elements.

Chapter 5
Interpreting Dream Images (2)

In the previous chapter, we practiced decoding dream images assuming they're symbols for something else. In this chapter, let's practice more, this time using real dreams.

Going Beyond the Surface Meaning

The following is a dream that fifteen-year-old John shared:

> "I was sitting in the backyard while babysitting my younger brother and sister after school. I was getting a little bored. Suddenly, this huge lion appeared out of nowhere and started to walk toward me."

Maybe you have also dreamed that something big and scary was approaching you. Often when people have this kind of dream, they interpret it as a sign that they are anxious about something or afraid of it on a subconscious level. That may be the case, but dreams are often trying to tell you about much more than your fears and anxieties. Many dreams are there to help you expand your horizons and show you different possibilities—about yourself, how to see things, how to deal with situations and so on. It turned out John's dream was such a dream, as you will see later.

Focusing on a Dream Image

As a start, let's practice decoding dream symbols by focusing on one element in a dream that stands out. It could be:

- ❖ an image, such as a big mountain, a sunset, a face, a scene from an event, a shape, etc.
- ❖ an object with special characteristics, such as a huge house, a vase with a strange handle, a very fast car, etc.
- ❖ a character, such as a friend or family member, a person you have never met, someone you used to know, an animal, a famous person, etc.

These dream elements are trying to get your attention. By exploring them, you can find out so much about a dream and its message. This is great news. Even if a dream seems confusing and complicated, you can pick one part of it to interpret to understand the message of the whole dream. So what do you think stands out from John's dream? There isn't one correct answer, but as you may have guessed, he picked "the huge lion" from the whole dream scene.

So in this case, one way to work on the dream is to focus on the lion and dig deeper to see what this huge lion really means for John and in his life.

Sometimes the dream character you need to explore is actually yourself. This is often the case if you dream you are doing something very special or unusual. For example, Olivia, whom I mentioned in the previous chapters, was a teacher in real life, but in the dream she was an actress performing on the stage in front of a large audience. In this case, we needed to explore further "Olivia as an actress" to understand the meaning of the dream.

Pay close attention to any dream element that stands out from the rest, as the standout element will often be the key to unlocking the dream's meaning.

How to Decode a Dream Element

As I said earlier, dream images are like secret codes standing in for actual messages. To understand the messages, you have to unravel the images and decode their special meanings, just like when you unwrap a package to see the gift inside. A simple way to decode a dream element is to ask yourself one or several of the following questions.

- **What could it symbolize? Is it a metaphor for something?**
- **What are the unique characteristics or "feeling-qualities" of the dream element? What is its essential energy?**
- **What is its unique power, if any?**
- **Does it remind you of someone or something? If so, what are its/his/her special qualities or characteristics?**

Answer in neutral and judgment-free words as much as possible. Remember, there is no right or wrong answer. The same dream image could have a different meaning for another person.

What did the lion in John's dream symbolize? Below is a conversation John had with a dream worker.

Dream Worker: So John, what do you think is the special energy, or quality, of the lion in your dream?

John: Well, it was really big and scary.

Dream Worker: Right, I understand it was scary for you in the dream, but try to remember once again how the lion actually came across to you. Describe for me its special quality or energy.

John closed his eyes for a moment and tried to picture the lion in his mind again.

John: I would say it had really powerful and confident qualities. Come to think of it, the lion was really cool. I wish I could be like that.

So there you have it. The dream image "huge lion" was actually about **"power and confidence"** for him.

Note that it was important for John to dig a little deeper than his initial reaction to the lion. He had to unravel the symbol to find the lion's essential quality and meaning. As you can see, the lion's theme of "power and confidence" was personally significant to John. He said he wished he could be like the lion. The dream was trying to let him know that "power and confidence" were important themes for him at that moment in his life, and he needed to pay attention to them. Since the lion was "getting closer" to John, it's possible that, symbolically speaking, the qualities of "power and confidence" were approaching him. Therefore, assuming this was a Your-Inner-World-Dream, one of the dream interpretations could have been as follows:

> John was beginning to know more about and possibly use his own power and confidence.

Now it's your turn to practice receiving a message from your dreams.

** Exercise: Message from the Dreamland **

Before you start, try the "Creating a Welcoming Space" exercise from Chapter 2, or just sit comfortably and take a few deep breaths.

1) When you are comfortable, slowly start to remember a dream you would like to understand. What does the dream feel like? Any special atmosphere? Just appreciate the dream for a few seconds.
2) Choose one element that stands out for you. It could be a character or its behavior, an image, an atmosphere, a specific color, or anything else that grabs your attention.
3) What is the element's special feeling-quality, or energy? See if you can describe it using a neutral, judgment-free word.
4) The dream is telling you the energy or quality you just extracted is somehow important for you. Ask yourself if the theme has been somehow playing out in your life.

You will learn more ways to understand your dreams in the following chapters, but just by learning the above method, you can already begin to interpret most of your dreams.

Write on a piece of paper the word of the energy or quality you got in the above exercise. Put it on the wall or carry it with you for the next few days and think about it from time to time. If the energy or quality is something new to you, don't forget to write it down in **Appendix A: The "New You."**

** Unwrapping the Secret Messages of Your Dreams **

Dreams are like wrapped gifts you receive every night. You must unwrap your dreams to get to their substance, just as you would unwrap a gift to get to its contents.

Remember, the same image can have a different meaning for a different person. For John, a lion symbolizes confidence; for someone else, a lion might mean leadership. If you are helping someone with their dreams, you always have to ask them something like:

"How would you describe its quality or energy?"
"How would you describe it for someone who has never seen it?"
"What could it be a metaphor for?"

Keep asking until you find a unique, personal meaning for the dreamer. As she discusses her dreams, she may suddenly remember an event in waking life, or a seemingly unconnected image may pop into her head. These thoughts are also important and could be the keys to understanding the meaning of the dream. Ask her more about these events or images and what qualities or energies they have.

The "Feeling" of a Dream

Dreamers are often asked: "So how do you feel about the dream?" Unfortunately, while this question may provide answers about the dreamer's emotional reactions, it may not help decode the dream itself. For example, if you asked John how he felt about his dream of the big lion (Chapter 5), he might say, "I don't know how I feel," "I feel confused," or "I feel scared." His emotional reactions would not necessarily contain constructive messages from his dreaming self.

If, on the other hand, you asked: "What does the dream (or the dream image) feel like?" you may get more useful answers that could help you understand the dream's meaning. As you saw in the previous chapter, when I asked

John the question this way, he was able to answer "power and confidence."

What about Scary or Unpleasant Dreams?

Do you remember I often asked you to describe the qualities of dream images in neutral, judgment-free words? Sometimes this may not be easy because the dream characters are scary or unlikeable, or simply because the dream is so mind-boggling. A useful trick is to imagine there is a transparent glass wall between you and the dream image. Through the glass wall, you can see the image clearly, but you are protected from it. From this detached perspective, try to capture the neutral quality of the dream element.

If you are still feeling too scared of the dream image to be neutral about it, don't worry. Set aside the dream for now, do the "Creating a Welcoming Space" exercise from Chapter 2, and wait for a less stressful dream to show up in the next week or so.

Chapter 6
Using Creativity and Imagination to Understand Dreams

Have you noticed how creative your dreams are? Sometimes they have characters beyond your imagination and storylines that are even stranger than the most outrageous novels and movies. Like your dreams, you have to be creative to understand them. So far, you have used words to explore the energies of dream images. There is another way to find out more about your dreams: drawing. Drawing captures the energies of dreams directly. You can use this method for any dream, but it also comes in handy when a dream image is too scary or mysterious to interpret in neutral, judgment-free language.

Remember John's dream of a huge lion? I asked him to draw the energy of the lion using colors matching its energy. Notice I said the energy of the lion, not a picture of the actual lion or the dream scene itself.

John closed his eyes and tried to remember what the lion's energy felt like. Then he started drawing with a black pen:

See how the bold, decisive sketch captures the confident and powerful energy of the lion. John enjoyed this exercise. Drawing helped him connect with the dream's strong energy.

Let's look at another example. Remember Jan's imaginary "dream" about a cake? She described the cake's basic qualities as "playfulness and happiness." Her energy drawing was very different from John's.

Now it's time for you to try. Grab a piece of paper and a pen or (even better) a set of markers, colored pencils or crayons.

** Exercise: Drawing Dream Energies **

1) Think of a dream image you want to understand and feel into its special energy and quality.
2) Using a color (or colors) matching the quality of the dream image, quickly sketch its energy.
3) Forget about the dream at this point. Look at the energy drawing. How would you describe it?
4) The dream is saying what you just described is a theme that is important for you in your life.

** Energy Drawing Tips **

- ❖ Draw the energy or feeling of the dream image, not the image itself.
- ❖ Don't think too much. Do it very quickly, not taking more than thirty seconds.
- ❖ Don't worry about your drawing skills. It's a doodle.
- ❖ Use colors to express the energy of the dream image, not necessarily the actual colors of the dream image.

When you have a dream that you can't describe with words or that leaves you with a vague impression, instead of writing about it in a dream journal, draw its energy. Feel free to use more than one color.

Chapter 7
Interpreting Dream Actions

So far, you have learned the basics of decoding dream images. The following methods will help you interpret more complicated dreams, where you are focused not only on images, but also on characters and their actions. For example, Lisa dreamed that her sister was flying. The dream left her with a lingering impression. To decode the dream, we followed these steps:

1) **Who or what is the dream character? ➜ Decode it.**

Lisa needed to first explore the meaning of "her sister" by asking herself, "What is her sister like?" and "What is her basic energy or characteristic?"

For Lisa, the basic energy of her sister was "openness."

2) **What is the dream character doing? ➜ Decode it**

In this case, Lisa's sister was flying. For Lisa, flying symbolized **"light-heartedness."**

3) **Put together the decoded words to get to the dream's meaning.**

Assuming the dream's message was about Lisa's inner self, and not about her sister, one meaning of the dream could have been:

> It was important for Lisa to be aware of a side of herself that could be very open. This side was, could be, or wanted to be light-hearted.

If Lisa wanted to know the message of the dream in more specific terms, she could come up with a few possibilities by thinking about her usual behavior.

For example, if she was usually very open to people and light-hearted, the dream could have been showing her that:

> Lisa could sometimes be too open and light-hearted and just flying away (instead of being down-to-earth, calm, practical, etc.), and she needed to be aware of it.

On the other hand, if she was usually the opposite of open (for example, a bit shy or withdrawn), the same dream could have been interpreted as follows:

Lisa needed to embrace the side of herself that was open and knew how to be light-hearted.

Either way, the dream was telling her, through the image of her sister flying, that it was important for her to be aware of something about openness and light-heartedness.

If the above dreamwork is too complicated for you, just stick to the simple method where you focus on an image that stands out in your dream. For example, focus on the image of "flying" or "your sister."

Could the Message Be for Someone Else?

Sometimes dreams about other people are actually about other people. For example, it's possible that Lisa's dream about her sister flying was not about Lisa's inner self, but about something happening in her sister's life. In other words, it was an Insight-into-Situation Dream, and Lisa's subconscious may have been telling her it was important to pay attention to what was happening to her sister. It's also possible that the dream was delivering messages both to Lisa *and* her sister.

Let's assume for now the above dream was meant for her sister. In that case, depending on how Lisa's sister usually was in reality, the dream could have been interpreted in different ways, such as:

- Lisa's sister had a tendency to be too open and just flying away, and she needed to be aware of this tendency.
- Lisa's sister had a side of herself that could be open and light-hearted, and it may have benefitted her to embrace this side more.

If you dream about someone you know and suspect the dream has a message for her, ask whether she is open to hearing about it. If so, share it with her. Be mindful of her feedback, and try not to force your interpretation on her. Remember, dream messages are personal, and there is no right or wrong answer.

Chapter 8
Mapping the Dream World

You have been learning how to understand your dreams in relation to your waking life, based on the premise that dreams are trying to help you understand yourself and your life better and from a wider perspective. Let's go further by learning how to understand your dreams in context.

Understanding Dreams in Context

In the previous chapter, I introduced you to the idea that the meaning of your dreams can vary depending on how you usually behave in your waking life. Here is a simple formula to remember:

> ➢ **If the quality of a dream image, character or behavior is *close to how you normally are in your life*:**

➔ The dream is saying you need to be more aware of this side of yourself. If you feel it's not serving you any longer, explore new ways to bring more balance into your life.

➢ **If the quality of a dream image, character or behavior is *different from how you normally are in your life*:**

➔ The dream is showing you a side of yourself that you haven't been aware of. Consider exploring this latent aspect of yourself.

If a dream leaves you with a lasting impression, it is inviting you to pay attention to a side of yourself, whether it's an old tendency you need to let go of or a potential you need to embrace.

Next time you have a dream that makes you wonder what it could mean, try to reflect first on how you are doing these days, and see if the dream could be a message for this aspect of your personality or your life.

Chapter 9
The Power of Dreaming

Everyday Mind and the Dream State

How is it that dreams can contain important messages for us? How are they different from normal thoughts? Think of it this way: During waking hours, you attention is more or less focused on taking care of your physical safety, planning a course of action, dealing with issues at school or work, calculating or measuring things, and so on. These are all important in order to get things done and lead your everyday life.

Now, when you go to sleep, your attention gets less focused as your consciousness expands. It's as though the door to a wider space were opening.

Some people say we are in touch with other realities when we sleep, and that our dreams contain information from these dimensions. Other people believe dreams are messages from our "higher selves."

Whatever the source of dreams may be, by being in this expanded consciousness space, you can access information that has skipped your normal awareness, such as:

❖ different perspectives on situations

- ❖ inner experiences and comprehensions
- ❖ creative solutions to problems
- ❖ artistic ideas
- ❖ insight on unexpressed or latent aspects of yourself, i.e., your inner potential

Dreams are filled with ideas, insight, learning experiences and opportunities for personal growth. By using the techniques in this book, you are training your everyday consciousness to accept and harness this wisdom.

Using Multiple Resources to Understand Dreams

So far, you have learned how to interpret your dreams using your own imagination and creativity. Another way to enhance your understanding of dreams is to read myths and fairytales. They often contain teaching and wisdom for self-transformation, as your dreams do. Knowing these stories may allow you to recognize similar themes and patterns in your dreams, and to understand what they could mean for your life.

You dream might also include a symbol that you haven't personally experienced. This image may be perplexing and difficult to understand. In this case, just appreciate the special feeling-qualities of the image. As you do so, a possible meaning may spontaneously pop into your head. If you are familiar with myths and fairytales, the meaning may come from that body of knowledge.

If you are still mystified, it's okay to forget about the image for a while and come back to it later. Many people who do this later come across books or websites that show, to their great surprise, exactly the same images, symbols or stories as the ones from their dreams.

Sacred Space and Dream Messages

Ancient peoples knew the power of dreaming. They went to sleep with the intention to receive messages and answers. In some cultures, such as ancient Japan and Greece, there were even special places and temples for receiving messages from dreams.

Maybe you can do something similar. Imagine your bedroom is a special temple to receive important messages. Arrange the room so that you feel relaxed and peaceful. It would be a good idea to turn off your TV and phone an hour or two before going to bed. Spend some time winding down, and remember to do the "Creating a Welcoming Space" exercise.

Before going to bed tonight, write down a question and put it on the bedside table. Say in your mind, "Tonight's dreams will answer my question." When you wake up, immediately record your dreams. Later, use the steps in this book to interpret your dreams and see if they give you some of the answers you're seeking.

** Dreams Are Doorways to Your Inner World **

Have you ever noticed that dreams are like plays or movies that feature different characters, images and atmospheres with fascinating storylines? Great stories, including myths and fairytales, teach readers a lot about their inner lives. Stories help us see things in different ways and guide us through our life journeys. For example, legends of heroic battles against monsters often teach us how to find courage and strength to deal with challenges. In the same way, many of your dreams are like fairytales and myths that are given to you each night to help you understand your inner world. Dream stories tell you about the different characters you have in yourself, the kinds of stories and dramas unfolding there, and possible ways to deal with your challenges. As discussed earlier in this book, dreams tell these stories in symbolical ways.

In a way, your personal growth is about gradually embracing these inner characters and qualities so that you will realize your full potential. In your everyday mind, the spotlight may be on one or two characters in your "inner theater," but dreams help you see what other characters and resources you may have that you haven't noticed before.

Chapter 10
Two Sides of the Moon

When you look at a full moon, are you looking at the whole moon? No. There is also the other side, the so-called "far side." It doesn't matter that you can't see the far side; it's still there. It's still a part of the moon.

People are the same. We all have a side that's a bit in the shadow; that is, we all have a side we cannot see so easily. Life is a journey of gradually discovering the unknown parts of yourself in order for you to be more whole. As you start to embrace these previously unknown parts of yourself, you will become able to see things from different perspectives and deal with situations in your life in more "rounded" ways.

How can you learn more about the unknown side of yourself? You guessed it. Pay attention to your dreams!

Noticing Different Qualities in Dreams

Some dreams show a side of yourself that is closest to your everyday self. Others show a less familiar side, including the inner resources and qualities that you haven't been using. Still other dreams show both at the same time through different images and characters.

For example, here is a dream that Sam, a twenty-year-old university student, shared.

> "I was in a red sports car with a guy I'd never met. He was the one driving the car, and I was sitting next to him feeling a little awkward and shy. We were on a highway, and he was driving very fast. I was worried we might have an accident, but I saw that he was a competent driver, and I soon began to enjoy the ride. "

How was this dream trying to show him different sides of himself? Sam saw that the main dream images and characters could be divided into two categories with distinct qualities:

1) Sam in the dream: quiet, cautious
2) The driver and his red sports car: powerful, competent, confident

When I asked Sam which one was closer to his usual self, he said he was definitely on the "quiet and cautious" side. The dream was showing him two sides of himself: the quiet and cautious self with which he was familiar, and the powerful, confident self that was less known to him. They were both important parts of the whole. He may have had this dream because the time had come for him to explore this other side of himself.

Dreams and Your Hidden Potentials

You might say, "What if I discover something bad about myself through my dreams?" If that happens, you will probably find that what seems negative at first is simply your hidden potential in disguise, and it could help you transform your life in positive ways. For example, a dream of missing a train may seem to be negative. However, if you are someone who tends to hurry too much, this dream may be showing you that you have the potential to take your time and go at your own pace.

Once again, if you don't feel ready to explore a certain dream or feel too overwhelmed, it's okay to wait until you feel safe or have another dream that is easier to interpret.

Chapter 11
Polarity Work

In this chapter, I will show you an easy and fun way to learn about seemingly opposite sides of yourself. This is a method called "Polarity Work" that we created for our Dream Cafe group. This exercise will show one of the main polarities, or themes, that you are dealing with in your life. The beauty of this method is that you can find two sides of yourself even when the dream is showing you just one side. Of course, there are more than two sides of yourself, so watch your future dreams to discover other sides to explore.

Polarity Work Step-by-Step

Let's use Amanda's dream as an example. Amanda, a popular and sociable high school student, shared the following dream:

"I was walking in a forest all by myself. Although I normally like going to places with my friends, I didn't feel lonely or anything in the dream. Then I came to a small but really nice open space surrounded by trees and flowers. I decided to take a break and sat on a tree stump. It was really nice to just sit there and hear the birds singing. "

1) Select any element that is interesting. → Decode it and write it on the left side of a piece of paper.

When I asked Amanda what was the most interesting thing in the dream for her, she said she really loved the whole feeling of the nice open space in the forest. She said its feeling-qualities were something like: **"peaceful, serene, quiet."**

I asked her to write these qualities on the left side of the paper:

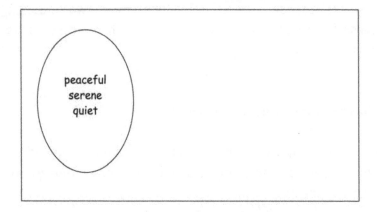

2) Imagine the Opposite Energy in Neutral Word. → Write it on the right side of the paper.

Next, I asked her to think of the opposite energies and describe them in as neutral words as possible. The opposite of "peaceful," "serene" and "quiet" for Amanda was: **"fun-loving, excited."**

I asked her to put these qualities on the opposite side of the paper:

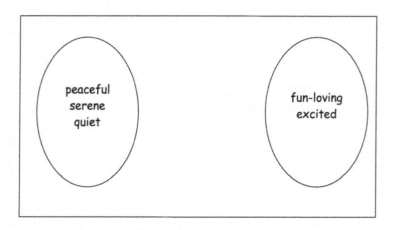

3) Connect the two polarities with a line.

I asked Amanda to draw a line to connect the two sets of feeling-qualities:

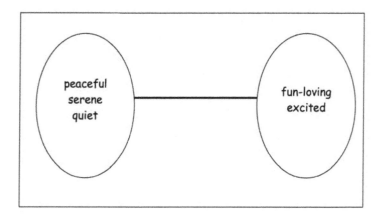

So there you have it. The two energies above are two sides that Amanda has. One of these sides is less expressed than the other, or more "in the shadow."

4) Mark where you are on the line.

I asked Amanda to mark where she felt she was along the line that connected the two sides:

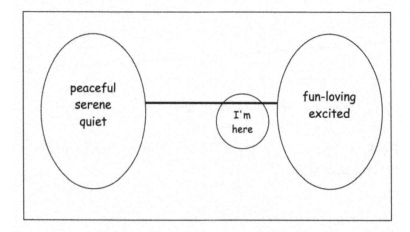

You can see Amanda considered herself to be much more excited than peaceful. By the way, it is rare to fall exactly in the middle of the line. Most people who do this exercise are closer to one polarity or the other.

5) Imagine what you could do to bring balance.

I asked Amanda what she could do to bring balance to these two sides of herself. She said she would start taking more time for herself. Although she loved hanging out with her friends, she sometimes felt a bit tired. She also had an idea to redecorate her bedroom to recreate the peaceful feeling of the forest. The last time I saw Amanda, she said she had continued connecting with the peaceful side of herself, and overall, she felt less tired than she did before exploring her dream.

Chapter 12
Creating Dream Masks

When you did the exercise in the previous chapter, were you surprised to find a hidden side of yourself? Did you already know a bit about it? You may have found it exciting or even impossible to accept.

In this chapter, let's take time to get to know this side of you a little more and make friends with it. You'll need a paper plate or a round piece of paper, some colored pencils or crayons, and the diagram you made in the previous chapter.

** Making Friends with the New You **

1) Choose the side further away from your usual self.
➔ Draw its energy on the paper plate.

Look at the two sides or energies from the exercise in the previous chapter. Pick the side that is further away from where you marked as "I'm here." If you marked "I'm here" in the middle, pick the side that interests you more.

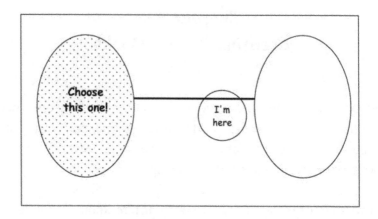

Now, on one side of the paper plate, draw its energy (just like we practiced in Chapter 6).

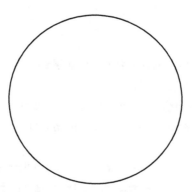

2) Try to get to know the energy.

Have a look at the energy drawing you made on the plate. How does it feel to look at it? Does it look familiar or not so much? Either way, try greeting it and saying hello.

Imagine it is a new friend you are trying to get to know better.

3) Draw a face embodying the quality of the energy on the other side of the plate.

Now comes the fun part. Imagine a character who embodies the feeling-quality of the energy. Draw the character's face on the other side of the paper plate. The face should have the same feeling-quality as the energy drawing. It doesn't have to be anything elaborate, although it's also creative and fun to use different materials.

Take a look at the mask Amanda made to express the "peaceful and serene" energy.

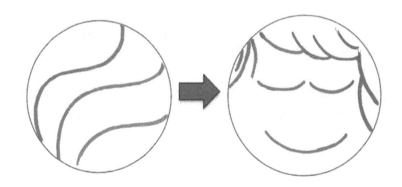

John made the following mask out of his shadow energy, "power and confidence."

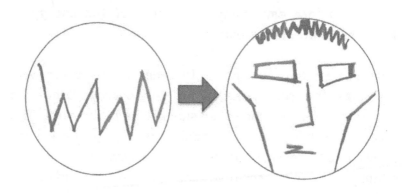

It's not about whether you can draw well. The important thing is that the mask is somehow expressing the energetic quality of the other side of yourself that you are trying to get to know.

4) Make friends with it. Imagine becoming this character.

Take a good look at your mask. Greet it again and feel its unique energy radiating toward you. If you feel like it, and when you are ready, try holding the mask in front of your face and pretending you *are* this character. You can make small eye holes and ear holes and attach a couple of rubber bands so that you can wear it. How does it feel to be this character? How does the world look from this perspective? What kind of life does this character have?

If you were this character, how would you deal with your problems? Does this character have a message for you?

For the next three days, place the mask where you can see it, maybe in your bedroom or living room. Try greeting it or wearing it every once in a while.

Chapter 13
Decoding Your Dreams: Step-by-Step Overview

Let's review the basic steps of dreamwork now. You can also find a concise version in Appendix C for a quick reference.

1. Before You Start...

❖ Reflect on Your Waking Life

Your dream may have a message or an answer for some of the situations you are dealing with in your life. Reflect on how you are doing lately in general. Do you have any deep questions that need to be answered? Is there any particular issue you are dealing with? Write them down if you like. Then set the paper aside and forget about it for now. We'll come back to it later.

❖ Create a Space to Welcome and Explore Your Dream

You can do the exercise in Chapter 2, or, if you don't have much time, take a couple deep breaths and just have the intention to welcome the dream and its message.

2. Identify Dream Type(s)

Once you've cleared the space in your mind, start remembering the dream's special atmosphere.

➤ If the most important thing in the dream is the feeling itself, it's a **Special Experience Dream** and the main message is:

  o "Just enjoy the feeling" or
  o "You need to take time to experience or explore the feeling more."

Try expressing the feeling-quality with neutral words or drawing it if you can. Ask yourself how you need this energy more in your life. Do a meditation to immerse yourself in this feeling and see if you get an answer to your questions from that place.

➤ If the dream has intriguing storylines, it's probably a **Your-Inner-World Dream** or **Insight-into-Situation Dream.** You need to decode the dream parts and images in the next steps.

➤ You may have a gut feeling that you just had a **Premonition Dream.** In that case, consider the following;

  o How would the event in the dream impact you or someone you know if it actually happened?

o If the dream feels like a warning about a situation you may encounter, take necessary actions or precautions.

o Even if it's a premonition dream, it may still contain some learning for you. Try understanding the dream as if it's your **Inner-World Dream** using the following steps if you can.

3. Identify Dream Image(s)

1) Summarize the whole dream or part of the dream.

Summarize the dream in a couple of simple sentences or a paragraph. If your dream is very long, choose the part that fascinates you the most.

2) Does it contain any universal themes or symbols?

Many dream symbols have the same meanings for almost everyone. Some of these symbols are explored in Appendix B: List of Common Dream Themes.

For example, a dream of childbirth almost always means something new is happening in your life. It may be that you are starting a new project or moving in a new direction.

If you don't think your dream contains any universal themes, move on to the next step.

3) Separate the summary into separate dream elements.

A dream is made of various elements, and each has a unique meaning. However, you don't have to analyze every single element. Just choose a couple that feel important. It's all right to focus on only one.

Dream elements may be:
> characters (including yourself doing something unusual or interesting)
> images
> objects
> events
> atmospheres or energies
> behaviors

4-5. Decoding Dream Images and Behaviors: What It Means for You

There are no strict rules for decoding dreams. Here are just a few ways to interpret different parts of your dream and how they all fit together. Remember, dreams are speaking to you in symbols, which are almost like secret codes. You need to break down the code to get to the deeper meaning. A tiger in a dream may not be about a literal tiger, but about courage, power or taking leadership, depending on how you see a tiger. Remember also that each part of a dream represents a part of you, including the parts you don't know so well yourself.

❖ Decoding Dream Images

If you are interpreting a dream image (for example, a person, object or scene), ask yourself one or several of the following questions:

- **What is its special quality, characteristic or energy?**
- **What do you think the dream image symbolizes? Is it a metaphor for something?**
- **Does it remind you of someone or something? If so, what is the feeling-quality or energy of that person or thing?**

Remember to use judgment-free, neutral words when you decode dream images. If it's difficult, use the drawing method in Chapter 6. If something seemingly unrelated mysteriously pops into your mind, like a memory or a scene from the past, decode those images in the same way you would decode a dream image.

➢ **If the quality of a dream image, character or its behavior is closer to how you normally are in your life:**
→ The dream is trying to tell you that you need to be more aware of this side of yourself. If you feel it's not serving you any longer or it has become a bit old, explore new ways of dealing with things to bring more balance.

> ➢ **If the quality of a dream image, character or its behavior is different from how you normally are in your life:**
> ➔ The dream is showing you the side of yourself that you haven't been aware of. Consider the possibility of exploring this latent aspect of yourself.

❖ **Decoding Dream Behaviors**

If you are trying to understand a dream scene where a character or an object is behaving in a certain way, you need to take an extra step.

1) **Who or what is behaving in a certain way?** For example, if you dreamed that your father was throwing away old clothes, you would start with "your father."

2) **What is the dream character like? What is the feeling-quality or energy?** Find out by using the method in Decoding Dream Images. For example, your father may represent "being hard-working."

3) **What is the dream character doing?** In this case, he was throwing away old clothes.

4) **What do you think the behavior or action symbolizes? Try describing it in a neutral term.** For example, "throwing away old clothes" could symbolize "letting go of the old" for some people. For others, it might mean "freedom."

5) **Put together your decoded words.**
Depending on your usual tendency, the dream could have different meanings:

> ➢ **The quality of a dream character is close to how you normally are in your life. / The quality of the behavior is also similar to how you would normally be.**

→ The dream could be inviting you to pay attention to this aspect of yourself and way of doing things. Is it still serving you to be and behave like this?

> ➢ **The quality of a dream character is close to how you normally are in your life. / The quality of the behavior is different from how you would normally be.**

→ The dream could be inviting you to start exploring new ways of being, behaving or dealing with things. For example, if you were hard-working just like your father but wouldn't have normally behaved as he did in the above dream, the dream could have been encouraging your hard-working self to relax a little and let go.

> ➢ **The quality of a dream character is different from how you normally are in your life. / The quality of the behavior is similar to how you would normally be.**

→ The dream is possibly showing you how to combine and balance the two qualities.

> ➢ **The quality of a dream character is different from how you are. / The quality of the behavior is also different.**

➔ The dream could be trying to show you an emerging aspect of yourself that can think and behave differently from how you normally think and behave.

Whether you need to release or embrace the qualities exhibited by dream elements, the dream is trying to tell you to pay attention to these aspects of yourself and acknowledge them.

❖ **Insight-into-Situation Dream**

If you feel your dream would make more sense if taken literally, the dream may not necessarily be about your inner world, but about your day-to-day experience. It's also possible that it's about both. For example, the dream of "my father throwing away old clothes" could have been about your subconscious picking up on what was happening to your father. In that case, depending on how your father was in real life, the dream could have been interpreted in different ways, such as:

- Your father tended to work too hard, and he needed to let loose (relax, let go of the old pattern, etc.).
- Your father tended to be too relaxed and let go of things too easily, and it was important that someone pay attention to it.

Many dreams contain symbolic messages about your inner world. However, if a dream seems to address specific situations or people in your life, see what happens if you interpret the dream more literally.

6. Apply Dream Messages to Your Life

Dreams give us messages, ideas and information that our waking minds have not yet processed. You can use this information to improve your life by opening to different perspectives and learning more about your potential.

As discussed earlier, dreams can help you in many ways:

> ➤ Dreams give you ideas, information or emotions that are difficult to notice while you are awake.
> ➤ Dreams show you where you are headed in your life.
> ➤ Dreams show you your potential.
> ➤ Dreams give you different perspectives on situations.
> ➤ Dreams help you become more creative.
> ➤ Dreams give you answers to your questions.

Once you understand what your dreams are trying to say, here are some questions you can ask yourself to start transforming your life:

> ➤ Has the dream given you clarity on a situation in your life? Remember the real-life situation you reflected on before you started interpreting the dream. See if you can deal with the situation or answer the

question using the new energy the dream has pointed out to you.

➢ Is your dream giving you hints on how to deal with an issue or project? Perhaps your dream is showing you how to see it from a different angle.

➢ Has the dream's theme been playing out in your everyday life? Think about the patterns in the dream. Are these patterns also present in the way you think and act, when you interact with others, or when you deal with issues? How about when you go about your school or work life? If the pattern has become old or no longer serves you, see if you can begin to let go of it.

➢ Is the dream showing you your inner potential in some way? What can you do to cultivate it?

➢ What can you do to bring more balance to your life? If you tend to use only one side of the polarity or one main pattern, try using the new energy the dream is showing you in a way that supports yourself and the people around you. (➔You can do Polarity Work in Chapter 11 to find out how.)

➢ Who would be good at living with these new qualities? Think of a real person or imaginary character who expresses the dream's energy. How would he or she deal with your situation? Create a polarity mask if it helps. (See Chapter 12.)

* * *

I hope this step-by-step overview to decoding your dreams has helped put together what you have learned to make some sense of your dreams. Some of the methods may seem complicated, but once you get the hang of it, you will be able to catch the messages of your dreams more quickly. Remember, you don't have to go through every single step all the time. Even doing only one or two of the above steps can go a long way toward understanding your dreams.

Afterword

I hope you have enjoyed learning how to tap into the magical world of dreams. Everyday there are more and more people around the world who, like you, become fascinated by dreamwork. Sometimes it helps to have a good listener who appreciates your dreams. I encourage you to share with your friends or family members who seem open to the ideas you have learned in this book. See if they are interested in chatting about dreams from time to time. You may also want to check if there is a dream group with an experienced facilitator in your area.

As mentioned in the introduction, my team and I offer groups called **Dream Cafe** in different parts of the world. Dream Cafe is a growing community of people who are interested in exploring dreams. We offer dream workshops held in a friendly atmosphere where participants can meet like-minded people. If you are interested, please check out the link below.

If you'd rather explore your dreams in private and would like a one-on-one session with an expert, please contact me using the following link, or find a qualified therapist in your area.

I hope you will continue making dreamwork a part of your daily routine and that doing so will give you growing sense of meaning and enchantment in your life journey.

<Links>

- **Dream Cafe London**:
  http://www.meetup.com/Dream-Cafe/
- **Dream Cafe International**:
  https://www.facebook.com/dream.cafe.group/
- **Technosophics, Ltd** :
  http://technosophics.com/home/dream-e/
- **Dreamwork sessions**: info@innerawareness.org

Appendix A
The "New You"

Whenever a dream points you to a new potential or energy within yourself, or you have an insight through exploring a dream, write it down on this page. You can also assign a page in your dream journal for this purpose. You can write a word, combination of words or a one-liner, e.g., "courage," "relaxation," and "Be more direct." You can also make small energy drawings.

Although I call these energies "new," they have always been a part of you, but you may not have paid attention to them until now. Read the list aloud or have someone read it to you from time to time so that you become familiar with it. In a way, what you write below will become your "mantra."

** New You: Your Mantra **

Appendix B
List of Common Dream Themes

Here is a list of common dream themes and their possible interpretations. These themes have relatively similar meaning for almost everyone. However, if they don't resonate with your dreams, forget the list and try the methods you have learned in this book.

Birth, baby, being pregnant

- New beginning
- Something new is about to come up in your life.
- You are getting in touch with your potential.
- You are in the process of change.

Carrying a baggage (or something big or heavy), carrying something and struggling

- Being burdened by something, e.g., your old pattern or a certain situation in your life
  - ➢ If the thing you are carrying is unusual and fascinating to you, try exploring the basic energy of it and see if it represents your emerging self.

Child

- New beginning
- Being childlike
- A part of yourself that is emerging, but still very new
  - ➢ Also ask yourself if the age of the child means something to you, e.g., what is three-year-old like in general? Did anything significant happen in your life at that age?

Clothes

- How you present yourself to others or in society. Decode the essential energy of the clothing.
  - ➢ See also "dressed."

Death, dying, being killed

- You are in the process of letting go of something in you (old pattern, etc.) before a new beginning.

Dressed, being inappropriately dressed, dressed in an unusual way

- The energy or quality of the way you are dressed (or someone else is dressed) represents your potential, hidden or emerging self.

Eating

- Nurturing yourself
  - ➤ Also look into the energy of the food you are eating in the dream. It may represent a new quality emerging in yourself that you need to integrate.

House, building, architecture

- A building often represents your inner self. Ground level is your conscious self; basement or hidden rooms are more subconscious parts of yourself; and the attic may represent a part of yourself that connects with inspiration, imagination or the spiritual realm. Explore the qualities of the building or the individual rooms to understand the dream in more depth.
  - ➤ See also "moving to a new house."

Moving to a new house, going to a new place

- Moving on to a new phase in life

Killing someone

- If the person has a similar energy to your everyday self, you could be letting go of something old in you before new beginning.

Naked, being naked

- Expressing yourself, revealing the true self
- It could mean that you are feeling too exposed and need protection or boundaries.

Name, ID card, passport

- Your identity. For example, losing an ID card suggests letting go of the current or perceived identity. A new self is emerging.

Person of the opposite gender

- May represent your inner feminine (if you are male) or masculine (if you are female)

Shoes

- What helps you go through or move forward in life

Vehicle, train

- What carries you through life. If the vehicle is unusual or surprising, the characteristics of the vehicle may represent your potential.

➢ See also "being on the road," "traveling," "losing control of a vehicle," and "changing train lines."

Being on the road, traveling, being in a vehicle

- Going through something in life
- Moving forward in life process

Losing control of a vehicle

- You feel you are losing control of a life situation, or not being in control in general, although you would like to be.
- The dream may also suggest you be more free, loosen your hold and be "in the flow."

Changing train lines

- Changing courses in life

Getting rid of something, letting go of something, losing something

- If that "something" represents something familiar or old for you, you are at a point where letting go of that kind of behavioral pattern, memory, or feeling is beneficial for you.

Coming closer, being together, talking to someone, embracing, being in love with someone

- Getting to know the part of yourself that is represented by that someone or something
- The other aspect of yourself is emerging.

Being chased by something or someone

- An aspect of yourself represented by the chaser is emerging. You don't know much about this aspect or are afraid to look at it.
- You are feeling overwhelmed by something in your life, but you haven't been aware of it.

Moving away, being separated

- Letting go of an old pattern in yourself.
- The dream may be showing what is happening on a subconscious level between you and another person or in this situation.

Appendix C
Step-by-Step Overview of Dreamwork

1. **Before You Start: Prepare for Dream Interpretation**

   ❖ **Reflect on your waking life.** Write down any question you want answered or situation you want to explore.
   ❖ **Create a space to welcome and explore your dream.**

2. **Identify Dream Type(s)**

   ➢ **Special-Experience Dreams** ➔ Take time to enjoy the feeling. Find out more using the dream decoding method or the drawing exercise.
   ➢ **Premonition Dreams** ➔ Take necessary actions. Try decoding it as a Your-Inner-World Dream.
   ➢ **Your-Inner-World Dreams** ➔ Go to Step 3.
   ➢ **Insight-into-Situation Dreams** ➔ Go to Step 3.

3. **Identify Dream Image(s)**

   1) **Summarize the dream or choose one part of the dream to interpret.**
   2) **Does it contain a universal image or theme?** ➔ Use the List of Common Dream Themes in

Appendix B. Fill in the gaps with the following steps.

3) **Break it down into individual dream elements,** e.g., characters, images, objects, events, atmospheres and behaviors.

4. Decode Dream Image(s)

Ask yourself these questions:

- What is the image's special feeling-quality, characteristic or energy?
- What do you think it symbolizes?
- Does it remind you of someone or something? What is the characteristic or energy of that person or thing?

Try drawing the energy to find out more.

Find the message(s). → The dream is trying to tell you the energy or quality you just identified is an aspect of yourself or life situation that needs your attention.

Keep playing. → Try Polarity Work (Chapter 11) to find out how this energy is important for your life and self-development.

5. Decode Dream Behavior(s)

Ask yourself these questions:

1) Who or what is behaving in a certain way?
2) What is the feeling-quality or energy of this person or object? (See Step 4).
3) What might this behavior symbolize?
4) Put together the decoded words.

Find the message(s). ➜ The dream is describing an aspect of yourself or your life situation that needs your attention.

6. Apply Dream Messages to Your Life

o Remember the situation in your life or question you had in mind in Step 1.
o Has the dreamwork answered your question or given you clarity about the situation?
o See if you can deal with the situation using the new energy the dream has pointed out to you.
o Try to express the dream's quality, i.e., your inner potential, in a way that benefits your life and the people around you.
o Ask yourself who may be good at being this way. Imagine how the person or character may deal with your situation. Try the mask exercise in Chapter 12 to feel this quality in yourself.

Appendix D
Dream-e:
Your Personal Dreaming Companion

I have worked with many people on their dreams over the years, and I've noticed that they often start understanding the meaning of their dreams just by having someone listen to them and ask some simple questions. Unfortunately, as the participants of my Dream Cafe group have told me again and again, it is often difficult to find someone open to discussing dreams in this way.

My partner Adi, a former NASA scientist and researcher in Artificial Intelligence who is also an experienced dream worker, suggested to create an A.I. technology to be released in the form of a mobile app that can serve as a dream companion or assistant. **Dream-e** is the result of our collaboration. It helps you record dreams and decode dream elements by asking you reflective questions, helping you solve problems using dream wisdom, and showing you your new, emerging qualities at a glance.

You can download Dream-e using the following link, where you will also find a few video tutorials on how to use it.

The Dream Compass

Deam-e link:
http://technosophics.com/home/dream-e/

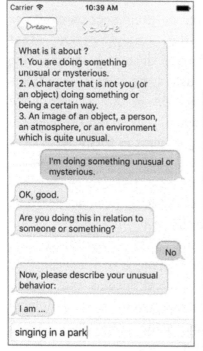

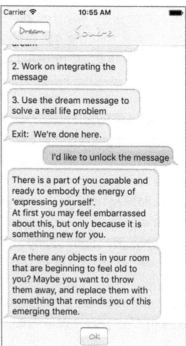

Bibliography

Joseph Campbell, *The Hero with a Thousand Faces*, Pantheon Books, 1949

C. G. Jung, *Man and His Symbols*, Doubleday, 1964

S. LaBerge, *Exploring the World of Lucid Dreams*, Ballantine Books, 1994

A. Mindell, The Dreammaker's Apprentice: Using Heightened States of Consciousness to Interpret Dreams, Hampton Roads Publishing Company, 2002

F. S. Perls, Gestalt Therapy Verbatim, Real People Press, 1969

R.A. Russo, *The Achuar: A Present-Day Dream People*, DreamTime magazine, IASD, Spring 2011, 28:2

Lightning Source UK Ltd.
Milton Keynes UK
UKHW03f2003220418
321436UK00001B/35/P